To

Amy & Joel

Woodard

With love from,

Kelly Scott

English Camp - 2004

Murska Sobota

May God Bless You!
I'll be praying
for you!

EVERY
MORNING
BRINGS
PROMISE

*A Celebration
of Hope*

William and
Patricia Coleman

SERVANT PUBLICATIONS
ANN ARBOR, MICHIGAN

Vine Books is an imprint of Servant Publications especially designed to serve evangelical Christians.

All Scripture references, unless otherwise indicated, are from the
HOLY BIBLE, NEW INTERNATIONAL VERSION.
© 1973, 1978, 1984 International Bible Society. Used by
permission of Zondervan Bible Publishers.

Published by Servant Publications
P.O. Box 8617
Ann Arbor, Michigan 48107

Cover design: Paul Higdon

99 00 01 02   10 9 8 7 6 5 4 3 2 1

Printed in the United States of America
ISBN 1-56955-164-2

Cataloging-in-Publication Data on file at the Library of Congress.

CONTENTS

PART THREE:
Failure Is a Launching Pad

PART FOUR:
Hope in One Hand—A Handkerchief in the Other

PART FIVE:
The Courage to Bounce Back

PART SIX:
Brave Enough to Dream

PROMISES
of HOPE *for*
EVERY
MORNING

We are going on——swinging
bravely forward along the grand
high road——and already behind
the distant mountains is the promise
of the sun.

Winston Churchill

*M*y eyes stay open through the
watches of the night,
that *I* may meditate on your
promises.

PSALM 119:148

When We Least Expect It

Driving out of Winona Lake, Indiana, early on a cold December morning, we headed toward the interstate. We were traveling to the East Coast to celebrate, with grandparents and other relatives, our child's first Christmas. We were a happy family, working our way through graduate school with an eye fixed on the future.

I drove. Pat sat in the backseat with two-month-old Mary.

As we rounded a bend leading out of town I felt the tires begin to slide. In another second the vehicle shot across the road, barely missing an oncoming car. Then we tore through a farm fence, and bounced violently across a field.

With one final lurch the car bounded into the air and landed on its side with wheels spinning. Few cars had seat belts in those days, and ours had none.

"Pat, where's the baby?" I yelled immediately. Pat did not answer. I struggled out of the car and could see my wife but no child.

Frantically rushing about I spied a blue blanket

wedged beneath the car. There was no crying to break the eerie silence. Not a sound came from the cloth that held our child's body. Kneeling, I cupped my hands and gently pulled out what I expected to be the broken figure of our dead baby.

As I turned Mary over to see her face, she let out the most beautiful scream I had ever heard. On her cheek were two small scratches. Her eyes were wide as saucers. The child reached out for comfort.

Pat and I bounded to the side of the road with our daughter. A kind couple stopped and rushed us to the hospital. Quickly the doctors examined Mary and before long released her, assuring us that she was fine.

Many babies have not survived auto accidents, and there is no reason why Mary did. Unable to explain it, we thank God that she is a grown mother today. The whys, hows, and what-ifs are all more than we understand.

I do know this: When I knelt down to pick up the blue blanket, I had no hope. But when I turned her over, hope beamed.

Sometimes when we least expect it, hope has a way of coming through. It doesn't have to make sense. But we sincerely thank God.

If Seeds Could Talk

No sensible seed could be happy on the day it goes into the dark, damp ground.

Odds are that the tiny grain has little chance of surviving such an ordeal. Normal hazards are staggering. Rains may flush the helpless seed out of its earthen bed and leave it exposed. A bird could stop beside the row and add the small speck to its dinner. Even the mindless wind might sweep down and carry the seed to a rocky place where it can't possibly hope to grow. As likely as not buried upside down, the little seed is totally at the mercy of fickle circumstances.

What if the rain does not come in sufficient amounts? What if the rain comes too late? A helpless seed could lie alone and perish in the ground with no means of promoting its own best interests.

But what if it manages to escape countless dangers and finds a safe place beneath God's rich earth? Who knows what possibilities wait there?

The seed's choices are clear:

First, it must accept what it cannot do. Dependent

on the help of others, the seed learns humility by waiting for rain and sunshine.

Second, it does what it can do. The seed adjusts itself and heads for the light. Finding its way through total darkness, this small grain heads upward.

Third, it believes that it can make it. Without the ability to see what's above ground, this seed starts its journey, one push at a time.

Because the seed is no quitter and it is willing to struggle, wriggle, and climb—because it believes what it cannot see—this tiny seed becomes a beautiful plant.

If seeds could talk, they would have tales to tell. Stories about darkness, doubts, and even despair. Stories about quietness, loneliness, and waiting. But they could also share hope. They could tell how their struggles were filled with meaning and purpose. And how good it felt to poke their pesky heads through the soil and know they were alive.

*N*ever yet was a springtime
when the buds forgot to bloom.

Margaret Elizabeth Sangster

Ten Things to
Thank God For

A new sunrise every morning.

The promise of a newborn baby.

A fresh spring after every winter.

The soon return of Jesus Christ.

A child's hand holding your finger.

The relief after pain goes away.

The ingredients for chocolate silk pie.

A red cardinal on the kitchen window.

A good belly laugh.

Slimy worms for fishing.

*R*efusal to hope is nothing more
than a decision to die.

Bernie S. Siegel, M.D.

*T*here is hope for a tree:
*I*f it is cut down, it will sprout
   again,
and its new shoots will not fail.

JOB 14:7

Just One Step

What does hope ask of me? Do I have to have a clear objective, unlimited resources, or a long-range plan? Need I work out a complicated scheme to navigate the many bends in the road?

That hasn't been my experience. Hope has merely asked that I take one small step at a time. One knock on a door, one phone call, one letter on its way. And when that small step is completed, I need take only one step more.

When I look at "the big picture" I become frightened. "What if this happens?" and "How will I handle tomorrow?" chase hope away. Trying to plan for all the what-ifs wears me down and leaves me in despair.

Hope sends a simple and direct command: Get up, stand up, and go.

Sometimes I have refused to try, for fear I might succeed. What if I run an ad and get a thousand calls? How will I fill that many orders? I have returned to the couch, exhausted at the very prospect of winning. I have put hope aside because

I am afraid it might actually work.

Hope doesn't demand more than I have to offer. It asks only that I dream a little. It asks that I be a bit daring, but only a bit. It challenges me to accept change, but only a few inches at a time.

Most of us can't sail around the world, but we can sail a few miles every day.

No one can paint the Capitol alone, but we can paint a little each day.

Do you ever count the pieces in a jigsaw puzzle before you begin to put it together? What if you fit the first 998 in place and then discover that two are missing? Most puzzle setters are willing to take that risk. You proceed by latching the borders, one flat edge at a time.

Hope does that. One piece of puzzle following another. Small pieces, one by one. There's no need to put it together all at once.

Ah, that's the reason a bird can

sing—

On his darkest day he believes in

Spring.

Douglas Malloch

*B*ut as for me,
I know that my Redeemer lives,
and that he will stand
upon the earth at last.

JOB 19:25, TLB

Blowing Up Balloons!

"**D**on't get your hopes up." That's Aunt Margaret's favorite saying. It's as though she is chief of the water brigade. Any time she sees a dreamer with a glowing flame, she runs forward with a bucket of water and douses the fire.

What is Aunt Margaret all about? Her husband died young, and for the next thirty years only a modest amount of money trickled in. Her children "turned out well," but they seldom return home. One might guess whether their mother's negative proverb dampens their desire to visit.

Margaret, like many of her ilk, doesn't mean any harm. She wants to help, or so she rationalizes. She wants to save others from the agony and pain of disappointment. "Don't get your hopes up" is her way of rescuing people from life's inevitable disasters.

It's a lot like telling a child not to blow up a balloon. After all, the wind might carry it over the fence and down the street. It might pop, and the noise would be startling. Eventually almost every balloon comes to no good end.

Never mind the joy that could come: Bouncing balloons from friend to friend, chasing balloons across the backyard.

"Fun and excitement aren't worth the risk," the prophets of doom remind us.

"Don't blow up your balloons!" That's what super-cautious people say. After a balloon is blown up, some dire result is certain to follow.

They are right.

If you stand up, eventually you will have to sit down.

If you marry, forty years from now your spouse might die.

If you purchase a television set, someday it will stop working.

If you buy an ice cream cone, someday you will need to buy another.

Pessimism is a choice. Some of us have chosen to fall in love with it. In turn we recommend pessimism to others.

Don't let the Margarets hold you down. As well-meaning as they might be, their philosophy is a drag. Go ahead. Blow up a balloon and buy an ice cream cone. You'll probably have lots of true satisfaction.

He has given us new birth
into a living hope
through the resurrection of Jesus
    Christ
from the dead.

1 PETER 1:3b

*In the midst of winter,
I finally learned
that there was in me
an invincible summer.*

Albert Camus

Soaring Like Eagles

Soaring high above for hours on end an eagle may cover a fifty-mile area, looking for a small creature. Fixing its incredible eyes on a rodent or a snake, the eagle effortlessly swoops down and silently picks up its helpless prey.

The power, speed, and majesty of this ancient bird caught the admiration of the prophets of old. Likewise, it leaves modern photographers and writers in awe.

Looking for a perfect image to convey strength when he felt weak, Isaiah wrote:

> *But those who hope in the Lord will renew their*
> *   strength.*
> *They will soar on wings like eagles;*
> *they will run and not grow weary,*
> *they will walk and not be faint.*

ISAIAH 40:31

Depression normally saps all energy out of us and robs us of any will to plod on. We simply want every-

one to go away, and we reject every opportunity.

The feeling of weakness causes spirits to become listless and sad. Our arms barely move and our legs feel like pillars of cement.

At our point of weakness the Bible offers tremendous encouragement. There is strength to be found in the Lord.

Not only does our faith allow us to stand, but soon we are able to walk and even begin to run. The Lord is able to give depressed persons new and exciting energy.

A depressed person may need counseling or education or time or even medication to help him or her along, but faith in a caring God also gives meaning to a life that has lost direction.

Inspiration is sometimes hard to come by. But think of an eagle stretching its wings and reaching for the sky. That sight reminds us that we do not have to succumb to despair, but by the grace of God it is time for us to fly again.

Hope ... means ... a continual looking forward to the eternal world.... It does not mean that we are to leave the present world as it is. If you read history, you will find that the Christians who did most for the present world were just those who thought most of the next.

C.S. Lewis

Two Kinds of People

The first kind are those
who check all the facts.
They buy books,
consult charts,
convene committees,
and become very well informed.

The second kind are those
who have a feeling,
who play a hunch,
who often like to say,
"Why don't we try it anyway?"

Group number one imagines
what might go wrong.
Group number two imagines
what might go right.

One carries an umbrella
in the car
just in case.

The other carries golf clubs
in the car
just in case.

In the best of all worlds
the two kinds finally meet.
Sort of like
"The Dreamer Meets the Accountant."
And without dumping cold water
on each other,
through some miracle of grace,
the Dreamer learns to count,
and the Accountant learns
to dream.

We need each other,
as hard as it is to admit.
Because it takes two kinds
to make tomorrow a better day.

*H*ope is the most pleasing passion
of the soul.

Eliza Haywood

HOPE *can* *get* YOU GOING AGAIN

If we were logical, the future would be bleak indeed. But we are more than logical. We are human beings, and we have faith, and we have hope, and we can work.

Jacques Cousteau

Pardon Me

Pardon me
If I failed
To listen to
Your dream.

Forgive me when I
Shut you off
Too soon.

I get wrapped up
In myself,
Anxious to tell
Only what I feel,
Only what I know.

Pardon me
For stepping on
Your words,
Your hopes,
Your faith,
Your joy,
Your stories.

Forgive me when I
Fail to reach
Outside myself
And hear
Your heart.

But I'm learning,
If ever so slowly,
To hear your hopes
And even to see
Your dreams.

Please don't stop.
Take a chance
Again.
Tell me of
The tune
You hum
Inside.

And I will grow
The richer still,
Seeing pictures
Drawn from
Your soul.

Tear the Roof Off

Tim collects brochures. He has a large cache of material about India, Alaska, China, and other exotic places. Tim has never traveled beyond his borders, but he fully intends to. He talks about travel, watches television specials, and becomes exhilarated at the thought of going places.

What he fails to comprehend is that hope is a verb. At its best, hope must be active to be alive. Taking action, putting dreams into motion, setting off a chain of activity—these show hope at its healthiest.

Too many of us sit alone, waiting for someone else to push us into activity. Deep in our subconscious minds we imagine that our friends will drop by and initiate contact. That kind of hope is merely a shadow.

Hope at its best is not passive. It doesn't expect a bus to drive into the living room and pick it up. Healthy hope goes out, flags down the bus, and takes off.

Paul had his eye on Sandy for a long time. He admired her at the office but never found the nerve to initiate a conversation.

After twisting, turning, and gyrating for nearly a year, he finally invited her to lunch. Instantly, Paul recognized what a fool he had been. A year's wasted energy could have been turned into a great friendship.

Paul had to put wheels on hope instead of expecting it to take off on its own.

The Bible tells about four men with a problem. They carried a paralytic friend to a house where Jesus was. Their hope was active. They were convinced the friend would be healed.

When they got to the house, it was so crowded they could not get in. Their hope was delivered a severe blow. Was it time to quit? Time to go back home? Or time to reorganize? The quartet decided to tear the roof off the house.

Hope went up on top of the building and dismantled the tiles (see Mk 2:4).

How long has it been since you tore the roof off a house to make your dreams come true? How long

has it been since you refused to let a barrier stop your parade?

Who tears the roofs off houses? Widows do it. Twelve-year-old boys do it. Businessmen do it. Housewives do it. It's not an art reserved for the bold or brash. It's the natural outcome for anyone who realizes that hope must be active.

Love ... always hopes.

1 Corinthians 13:6-7

Yesterday is experience.

Tomorrow is hope.

Today is getting from one to the

other as best we can.

John M. Henry

Hope Till the End

The doctor broke the sad news. Marge's cancerous condition was widespread and terminal.

"How long?" she wondered.

"Two years at the outset," he replied solemnly.

"I have a great deal to get done," Marge told her worried family. "I'm making a dress for Annie's graduation. I promised to teach a class in the fall."

"Of course," said her sister in a cautious tone, "but first you must get some rest and build up your strength."

"I don't have time for that," Marge continued. "I refuse to just lie here and worry about my blood count. There must be some way to stretch my time to three or maybe four years. Besides, doctors are wrong half the time. I'm getting out of bed."

Marge's optimism and drive became contagious. The more she laid out plans for tomorrow, the more her relatives jumped on the bandwagon. Her hope became their hope.

The cancer didn't go away, but its spreading slowed. One day Marge put the question to her doc-

tor squarely. "Don't you think I can hold on for four years instead of two?"

"If anyone can, I believe you can."

"That's all I needed to know."

She didn't deny the cancer but neither did she bow down to it. Marge turned a spark of hope into a flame.

Fortunately those around her did not resist her hope. Courage is hard enough to hold onto; and if one must hold it alone, the grief can be unbearable.

Despite Marge's determination and industry, the destructive cells would not be denied forever. After three and a half years she lay helpless in bed. Looking at the handful of people who stood by her bed, Marge whispered, "It's time to go." That night she died.

When people choose to hope, their friends are wise to join in the dream. Good friends dare not put up obstacles or argue with optimism. Likewise, we do friends a favor if we do not disagree when they give up on hope. Each individual knows best when to hope and when not to.

*Lay aside life-harming heaviness
and entertain a cheerful disposition.*
    Bushy, in William Shakespeare's
            King Richard II

*R*eturn to your fortress,
O prisoners of hope;
even now *I* announce
that *I* will restore twice as much to you.

ZECHARIAH 9:12

Health and Expectation

Recently a doctor told me his primary role is that of a coach. Sure, he went on to explain, he writes prescriptions and he schedules all the necessary procedures, but that isn't the entire matter. Basic to care is his ability to encourage and inspire the patient to expect to get better.

There is an underlying principle about health that says those who don't expect to get well often do not. And those who proceed as if they are getting strong generally do.

Examples of health and expectation are too plentiful to ignore. Evidence abounds that many people get better because their doctors tell them they will. Some probably also get worse if their doctors predict it.

A psychiatrist from Connecticut went so far as to say, "If you expect to get better, you will." He also said that placebos, such as sugar pills, are about half as effective as real medicine.

In one study a group of patients who were allergic to poison ivy were told their arms were being

rubbed with a nonpoisonous leaf. In fact, the leaf *was* poison ivy. Of the thirteen who were rubbed with the leaf, eleven did not break out in a rash. Because someone told them it was not poison ivy, they believed.

None of us should be foolish. If we are sick, we should see a doctor. If we are taking medicine, we should continue to take it. But we should also realize that expectation can play a large role in what might happen.

The person who says, "What's the point? I won't get better anyway," might work against his own recovery.

Expectation does not suspend the laws of nature. All of us die, no matter how optimistic we might be. But some of us live a little longer and live a little better because we have the "want to."

The hours we pass with happy
prospects in view are more pleasant
than those crowned with fruition.
In the first case we cook the dish
to our own appetite;
in the last it is cooked for us.

Oliver Goldsmith

*F*rom: Paul, a missionary of Jesus Christ, sent out by the direct command of God our Savior and by Jesus Christ our Lord——our only hope.

1 TIMOTHY 1:1, TLB

*T*o eat bread without hope
is still slowly to starve to death.

Pearl S. Buck

Nocebo and Placebo

We have probably all heard of the placebo effect. That's when a doctor gives us sugar pills and calls them medicine. Because the doctor tells us we will get better, we do. Believing has a healthy effect on us.

Only recently have I been introduced to the word *nocebo*. If someone you trust tells you things will go badly for you and you believe that individual, things are more likely to go sour.

Simply put, this means that if you believe something bad is going to happen, it is far more likely to come true. If a physician says it will take seven days to get over a cold, you are probably not going to shake it in three.

That's why you need to be careful whom you trust. If a parent kept saying you could never make it in college, there is a fairly good chance you didn't do well in school. You bought into the negatives and never mastered learning.

How many of us have friends who keep taking the promise out of life by slipping us nocebos? Someone who says,

"You'll be sorry."

"You won't be able to do the work."

"The climate will make you sick."

Inevitably we end up sorry, discouraged, and sick.

Those disparaging friends didn't chain our hands or lock us in boxes, but their words had great force.

"You're going to make a fool of yourself." A nocebo.

"You're going to lose money." A nocebo.

"You'd better stop dreaming." A nocebo.

"Aren't you getting old for that?" A nocebo.

"Boy, you never learn." A nocebo.

"Everybody has tried that." A nocebo.

Somewhere in the cabinets of our minds we might have a large bottle of nocebos. And maybe we've been generously distributing them. Who can tell how many people we have made sick and gloomy because we handed each of them one nocebo too many.

Give it a serious look. Are we accepting nocebos too easily and swallowing them too readily? Are we handing them out a bit too freely? Let's toss them in the trash.

*T*here is no better or more blessed bondage than to be a prisoner of hope.

Roy Z. Kemp

Ten Keys to Optimism

Admit that life is tough.
Be realistic. Don't pretend troubles don't exist.

Accept the good side of life.
Make a list of what you enjoy and find satisfying.

Is it a fact or a feeling?
Are things really bad, or do they just seem that way?

Be willing to fight the odds.
People who discourage easily are discouraged most of the time.

Surround yourself with upbeat people.
If you hang around with defeatists, you feel defeated.

Pessimism is paganism.
Those without hope have lost sight of God's potential.

Optimism is a Christian experience.
Hope is at the center of a spiritual life.
Optimism believes that God cares.

Be careful of the message you send.
Hope vanishes if you keep sending negative messages on your fax machine.

Don't be optimistic about everything.
This is unrealistic, unkind, and exhausting.
Some things simply won't work.

What would you like to do?
If you could let go and enjoy life, how would you go about it?

Now ask yourself: Who is optimistic and who is pessimistic?
Why do we become one and not the other?

There Were Good Days

Lisa and Roger felt as if the foundation had dropped out of their marriage. When they went for counseling, they were barely talking. Neither could remember a reason to stay together. Everything seemed bad.

With a bit of prodding and a hint or two from the counselor, they soon began to recall a good day here and a couple of good days there. Their past began to change from black to gray. A few stories later the picture lightened up considerably.

Once they admitted that there had been sunshine in the past, that sunshine started to spill over into the future. Because they had enjoyed each other before, hope began to rise that they could enjoy each other again.

The same principle applies to darkness. If we believe everything has always been dark, a shadow tends to cast itself over our tomorrows.

Whether we're discussing marriage, business, parenting, or trapshooting, the rule is the same. If the sun has shone before, there is a good chance it could

shine again. Hope can be found by looking behind us as well as by looking ahead.

The hopeless tend to say things like "I've never amounted to anything" or "I always messed things up." A person who says that isn't telling the truth; and once he starts lying to himself, more lies are likely to follow. The first key to progress is taking a pledge to tell yourself the truth. And the truth is: There have been good and satisfying accomplishments.

Remember the day when you took the test and even you were surprised at how well you did? Can you recall the time when you refinished a desk and what a professional-looking job it was? What about the weekend you helped paint an elderly couple's house? You didn't always feel useless. And that means you don't have to feel that way in the future.

Every fulfilled dream makes the next dream possible. Every goal reached makes the next more likely. Life is a series of building blocks, and each one put in place makes the foundation stronger. Remembering our successes gives us hope.

You can't massacre an idea.
You cannot run tanks over hope.

Ronald Reagan

FAILURE *is a* LAUNCHING PAD

Beware how you take away hope from any human being.

Oliver Wendell Holmes

*F*or a just man falleth seven times, and riseth up again.

PROVERBS 24:16, KJV

Good News About Failure

Anyone who hasn't had the pleasure of failure has not yet begun to live. Many of life's finest qualities can only be realized after we have been fired from a job, failed a math test, or been rejected by that special someone.

There are no shortcuts. Being valedictorian, homecoming king, and captain of the football team all rolled into one will not substitute for the unique rewards gained by one genuine failure. Heart-wrenching, disgusting, dirt-eating failure.

But be of good cheer. It's going to happen. And the sooner the better. Someone will look you in the eye and say, "Don't come back." Someone will review your job evaluation and note, "This person is uniquely *unqualified* for this position."

As unlikely as this sounds, the person who rejects you will at that moment be doing you a first-class favor. Better than a raise. Greater than a hug. Far more valuable than winning the lottery.

Because through that act of failure you will be forced to ask yourself who you are and what you

believe. No long string of victories could ever make you do that.

And the good news about failure is that most of us will become better people because we flunked or were rejected.

If we are willing to put our faith to work, we will learn the big lesson the apostle Paul learned. Instead of giving Paul good health, God taught him this valuable truth: "I am with you; that is all you need. My power shows up best in weak people" (2 Cor 12:9, TLB).

That's something none of us can learn by becoming the CEO or secretary of state or champion lumberjack. We only learn how God uses weak people when we come face to face with our own weakness.

So don't let failure frighten you so much. Go ahead, bowl a forty-two. Get dragged through the mud on a tug-of-war team. Be the poorest salesman in your district. And remember that God loves us weak people down to the bottom of our toes.

*C*risis: opportunity riding on dangerous winds.

Chinese saying

*T*he only true failure
is the failure to try.

Dancing With God

He was so tired ruts gutted his face. Like old leather, his cheeks sagged, and his eyes stared as if they no longer wanted to see.

"What really is the point?" he asked out loud. The tone of his voice suggested that he didn't believe an answer existed.

"My wife has left me. My finances are a mess. My health is going downhill. Soon they're going to fire me for not coming to work."

It was all true. There was no sense in telling the forty-five-year-old mechanic to buck up. Things really were a shambles.

Understandably, he had forgotten how to dance with God. No longer could he hear music. Empty and without energy, he was sitting next to the wall. From all appearances the dejected man might sit out the dance forever.

What he had forgotten, if he ever knew it, was that when we dance with God we need to dance the one-step. Nothing fast. Nothing fancy. Merely a slow, calm movement, one step at a time.

Believers don't have to see tomorrow, next week,

or even beyond. They don't have to understand how it will all "come together." That's why they call us believers.

The one-step means we will simply place one foot in front of the other. That's all the faith we need. One step in front of the other. We don't have to see where step ten or step one hundred might lead us. God dances forward, sometimes sideways, and we dance best when we dance at his speed.

Up and off the chair. Take the first step. Get dressed. Eat a piece of toast. Head out the door. What will you do when you get there? Take care of that when you arrive. Keep moving. That's how the dance is patterned.

It's hard to dance sitting down. Even harder staring at the floor.

What if we fall down or look awkward stumbling across the floor? Sometimes we forget that God is by our side, holding our hands and dancing with us. That makes all the difference.

The fact that God has prohibited despair gives misfortune the right to hope all things, and leaves hope free to dare all things.

Madame Swetchine

May the God of hope fill you with all joy and peace as you trust in him, so that you may overflow with hope by the power of the Holy Spirit.

ROMANS 15:13

Ten Reasons to Hope

I cut my finger and the skin is healing.

I owe less money than I did last year.

My medical insurance actually paid a bill.

Twenty-three children get off the school bus in front of my house.

After a flood cleanup, my state returned a $3 million surplus to the federal government.

The number of major crimes is down in our nation.

A scientist announced that we are three-quarters of the way toward discovering a cure for cancer.

A factory in my county discovered that they had overpaid their property tax. They told the county to keep the extra money because the schools need it.

Children with leukemia are far less likely to die from the disease than they used to be.

Young people continue to acknowledge their faith in God in high numbers.

*T*he latest definition of an
optimist is one who fills up his
crossword puzzle in ink.

Clement King Shorter

The Gift of "Gushing"

I used to try and encourage everyone. "Don't worry," I would say, "your sick grandmother will be just fine." Two days later she would die. Or I'd say, "I have a feeling that next week you are going to get that new job." A couple of weeks later my friend would be in line at the food bank.

Eventually I decided that what I called encouragement was actually "gushing." Automatically I rattled off platitudes of empty, even hollow bubbles that meant nothing. Along the way I probably hurt as many people as I helped.

The gift of gushing doesn't have a divine origin. It is a role we take on without taking a close look at what we're doing.

It is wishful thinking that says, "Don't worry, everything will turn out swell."

Encouragement, on the other hand, says, "However things work out, I believe you can find strength, in God, to go on."

Or, even better, it says, "Remember, if you don't get the job Tuesday, I'll still help you with groceries." Or, "I realize the operation may not go well,

and if it doesn't, you can count on me to help with the kids."

In our best moments we offer our courage to people who have lost their courage. We may have to do that until they are able to find theirs again.

Job's idea of courage was "Though he slay me, yet will I hope in him" (13:15a). He knew things might not get any better, but he could find strength even in loss. The New Testament tells us to encourage one another daily (see Heb 3:13).

Every now and again we meet someone who is walking the thin line of deep discouragement. At any time he might dip into the dark waters of despair. We do the work of God when we reach out and shine a light toward the shore.

*H*ope is when your hands and feet keep on working when your head says it can't be done.

Ten More Things to Thank God For

The promise of a new day.

Guardian angels.

The sweet smell of rain.

That he put the story of Job in the Bible.

White snow covering everything.

Clouds of many shapes and colors.

A land where there will be no tears.

Whoever invented spot remover.

Elastic bands in clothes.

The promise of a home in eternity.

I do not believe that true optimism can come about, except through tragedy.

Madeleine L'Engle

By day the Lord directs his love,
at night his song is with me—
a prayer to the God of my life.

PSALM 42:8

HOPE *in* ONE HAND— A HANDKERCHIEF *in the* OTHER

Hope is the thing with feathers that perches in the soul.

Emily Dickinson

*H*e will not break the bruised reed, nor quench the dimly burning flame. *H*e will encourage the fainthearted, those tempted to despair. *H*e will see full justice given to all who have been wronged.

ISAIAH 42:3, TLB

Wiggle Under the Wings

Thursday morning was the pits for Larry.

When he read the paper, he couldn't figure out whether stocks were up or down. Frustrated, he washed his glasses but the blur didn't go away.

It took fifteen minutes to find the car keys. By the time he got to the office, his condition was obvious to him. His body wasn't working, his mind couldn't focus, and his hair refused to lie down. Larry knew his best hope was to stay cool and try to coast through the day. If he remained calm and kept smiling, eight hours might pass without too much damage.

It happens. And when it does, no amount of optimism will help. Nothing will jump-start the battery. "Creative thinking," "bouncing back," "zestful thrust," and all the other optimistic phrases are useless. Some days life isn't going to come together. Shift down to neutral and try to coast.

The problem with an overload of motivational literature is that we begin to believe we are omnipotent.

We think we always have enough power at our cores. Forget it. Some days the old crank won't turn. Once in a while we have to sit in the backseat and wait.

Those are the days when we meekly ask God to lift his wing. Then, like the psalmist, we wiggle beneath the feathery limb and quit trying. We snuggle in close to the soft side and sigh in relief as the wing drops protectively over us.

That's all we need for now. The smart ones stay there until the storm passes. Only then do they come out and take on the world again.

Wiggling under God's wing is no disgrace. Staying there will degenerate into escapism. But it's a great place to visit.

All of us can think of a time when we should have gone there, but we were too stubborn. Because we were boneheaded we pressed on. We chewed out our teenagers. We broke objects we were repairing. When in trouble, we canceled our engagements with friends who cared.

Too proud to wiggle under the wing, we stayed out in the storm as the wind raised havoc.

"O God, have pity, for I am trusting you! I will hide beneath the shadow of your wings until this storm is past" (Ps 57:1, TLB).

Hope, like faith, is nothing if it is not courageous; it is nothing if it is not ridiculous.

Thornton Wilder

*H*ope is the parent of faith.

C.A. Bartol

Don't Get Your Hopes Up

Taxes aren't going to go away.

Spinach is always going to taste that way.

Infants will always want to be fed
at 2:00 A.M.

Teens will always play music loudly.

A second dish of ice cream will always
be fattening.

There will never be another movie
like your favorite one.

Your husband won't like musicals
or love stories.

Your wife will probably never
understand football.

Teens will always shout,
"You just don't understand."

You will probably always be a few pounds overweight.

You will never get many dollars ahead.

Every golf shot will be a disappointment, except the one that goes in the cup.

For Such a Time as This

Hospitals weren't her thing. Neither were late-night plane rides or dark airports on rainy nights. But there Megan stood, hailing a taxi, hurrying to a bedside.

Riding through the streets of Houston gave the young businesswoman time to think. *This is all so unpredictable and out of control,* she protested to no one in particular.

"Please hurry," she told the cab driver. "My aunt could well be dying at this very moment."

Arriving at her destination, Megan quickly paid the driver, only to hear him say, "Thanks, lady. I'm glad God let you come here for such a time as this."

Startled, she mumbled a reply and walked toward the hospital's revolving doors.

"For such a time as this," she repeated to herself. "I never thought about that. Could it be that God has me here for such a time as this?"

It isn't often that we rush toward hard times. More frequently we want to run the opposite way. That's the human condition. We don't usually run

toward accidents or suffering.

But sometimes we know God must have put us here for more than just the good times. Life has to be more than carnival rides, birthday parties, and afternoons at the beach. We are also here for the special times when we need to reach out and touch those who need us.

When Queen Esther's people were in trouble, Mordecai told her that maybe God had put her in the palace for just such a time as this (see Est 4:14). She now had the opportunity to reach out and help.

Children may need us. Coworkers might call us for help. The elderly could long for a listening ear. And in those moments we might ask ourselves if indeed God has put us here for just such a time as this.

*Hope is the feeling you have
that the feeling you have isn't
permanent.*

                              Jean Kerr

Why are you downcast, O my soul?
Why so disturbed within me?
Put your hope in God,
for I will yet praise him,
my Savior and my God.

PSALM 42:5-6a

Magic Glue

I wish I had some magic glue;
I know exactly what I'd do.

I'd paste some hearts
And make them mend
So parents would never
Choose to fight again.

For guns of war
Both large and narrow
I'd drop some glue
Right down each barrel.

And for angry people
Who are mean and vile
I'd paste their cheeks
And make them smile.

For every child
Who cries alone

I'd stick a picture of Jesus
On his telephone.

Onto everyone
Filled with prejudice
I'd paste a red
And rosy kiss.

I wish I had some magic glue;
I know exactly what I'd do.

Hope is the power of being cheerful in circumstances which we know to be desperate.

G.K. Chesterton

Pandora's Box

According to legend, Pandora was a Greek princess who received a precious gift. The gods gave her a box but told her never to open it. Jealous of her beauty and charm, they actually wanted Pandora to make a fatal mistake and lift the lid.

Understandably, the princess became overwhelmed by the twin calls of curiosity and temptation. As Pandora cracked open the chest to steal a quick look inside, the great tragedies of life came racing out. Disease, maladies, and even madness escaped the box and ran rapidly throughout the world.

Fortunately Pandora grasped one good quality before she closed the box. The princess was able to grab hope.

Imagine what life would be like if only disaster, heartbreak, and illness were allowed to roam the earth. How terrible would be our existence if we could find no hope to offset our afflictions.

Pain, grief, and disappointment are not choices. They are loose in the world and bring their havoc whether we want them to or not. But hope *is* a choice.

Hope is a decision that each of us either accepts or rejects. Suffering is not an option, but hope clearly is. We choose to believe we will overcome, or else we choose to believe that we cannot.

Every day we get to decide again. If heartache is free to attack whomever it wishes, if Pandora's box has been opened, how foolish we would be to let the gift of hope float away.

*H*ope is like the sun, which,

as we journey toward it, casts the

shadow of our burden behind us.

S. Smiles

God is our refuge and strength,

an ever-present help in trouble.

PSALM 46:1

It's Time to Change

Diane believed in change. She had seen her cousin, Andy, change. Previously his terrible temper had made him miserable to be around. But when his wife threatened to leave him, Andy woke up, sought help, and today is entirely different.

That was a fact that Diane couldn't argue with. Diane believes in change for others. The trouble is she doesn't believe in it for herself.

Many of us feel the same way she does. Change is for others. As for me, I am stuck with the cards I have been dealt. Or sometimes the hand I dealt myself.

Consequently we stand pat. We don't draw more cards. We seldom throw any away. We would rather sit still even if it means we are going to lose. Big time lose.

To dream of change is to envision a better, brighter tomorrow: living with less pain, less disappointment, and less sadness. Change might mean new friends and new opportunities. Change could mean an improved and much more pleasant me.

Change is risky. Any movement risks the chance

of getting hurt. That's why we fear change. But there is also the possibility that the new me could be very fulfilling.

If change seems like something we want, there are two ways to go about securing it. One is by ourselves. The other is with someone else.

We have all seen people who quit smoking, lost weight, or learned to speak in public all on their own. The potential to create personal change is enormous and understandable. But many of us have tried this route only to end up lost and eventually to circle back to where we started.

A second avenue leading to change is to get someone to help: a cousin, a counselor, a friend, or chance acquaintance. Someone who will listen and offer a bit of guidance. Not someone who will take over and try to run our lives.

After all, God often uses people to change us. When someone points us in a better direction, maybe we need to pay attention. This could be the very person the Lord has sent along to give us a nudge.

*It has been said that no man ever
sank under the burden of the day.
It is when tomorrow's burden is
added to the burden of today
that the weight is more than
a man can bear.*

G. MacDonald

The COURAGE to BOUNCE BACK

It is impossible for that man to despair who remembers that his Helper is omnipotent.

Jeremy Taylor

*B*ut encourage one another daily.

HEBREWS 3:13a

A Dozen
Hopeless Sayings

Are any of these favorites of yours?

If it can go wrong it will.

It's always darkest just before it gets black.

The average person doesn't have a chance.

It's all political.

You can't fight city hall.

You can't trust anyone.

Nothing ever works out anyway.

What's the use of trying?

They never listen to someone like me.

You can't win.

If it isn't one thing it's another.

Why don't I eat worms and die?

The first qualification for a physician is hopefulness.

James Little, M.D.

Belief in God, Belief in Me

In order for hope to work, we must believe in something. To put hope into gear, we need a goal that we believe is possible, even if the possibility is small and foggy.

If we must first believe, where do we place our faith? There seem to be three choices:

1. We can believe in God.
2. We can believe in ourselves.
3. We can believe in both.

The best route to go is the last one.

A person who sits on a log and waits for God to do something is merely a lump that breathes. The person who believes that God helps him gets off the log and goes to work.

If we believe in God but have no faith in ourselves, the burden is too heavy. To declare ourselves worthless is fake humility. We are all capable of doing things. We can thank God for that ability.

Hope forms a partnership. We take hold of our

potential and ask God to help us carry it out. We find strength by asking for guidance and assistance.

The psalmist tells us, "Be strong and take heart, all you who hope in the Lord" (31:24). He doesn't say, "Be weak, give up, and let the Lord take over."

God seems to accomplish more in people who are actively serving him. Let the plans go forward. The Lord works well on a team even if he is the controlling partner.

*And his name shall be the hope
of all the world.*

MATTHEW 12:21, TLB

*D*iscouraged people
have lost their courage.

A Bad Century

That's what the message on the T-shirt said: "Chicago Cubs—Any Team Can Have a Bad Century." What kind of faith does it take to be a Cubs fan, anyway? What kind of person, at the end of a 162-game season, can raise his hand and yell, "Wait until next year"?

Inside he knows better. They aren't going to be champs next year either. But a tiny glimmer inside says, "Who's to say? It could happen."

Of course it can. If dogs can be carried twelve hundred miles from home and still find their way back ... if cicadas can wait seventeen years before showing their faces and joining in their insect orchestra ... if Halley's Comet can make the big loop and return in seventy-six years ... can't we keep our faith until our own dreams come true?

Faith means what we believe in can come true. Faith means we believe in tomorrow.

In an impatient world, waiting isn't a favorite theme. We don't like to stand in the checkout line or wait for a new car or a better paying job. Instant gratification seems the only way to go.

Most of us have a bad year now and then. We might have two bad years. Those of us who accept that as part of the life cycle are the ones who can best wait for the sunshine.

We all can go through a wilderness experience. For a while we wander around with little direction. Part of the time we feel lost. Sometimes we feel as if we are going in circles. Why doesn't our path become clear? No amount of pleading with God seems to bring us out into the open.

Wilderness sloshing may be good for a while. Walking aimlessly could be character building. The silence of God might even be instructive.

Down days, down months, down seasons are OK. Pull in your belt. Pull up the collar on the back of your jacket. Hold on to God's promises. Wait till next year.

*A*fter all, tomorrow is another day.

Margaret Mitchell,

Final line of Gone With The Wind

It Takes Courage

It takes courage
To stand alone
When no one else
Seems to care.

Courage to speak up,
Courage to raise your hand,
Courage to show
A better way.

When there are few
Who can see
A brighter tomorrow,
And fewer still
Who want to reach out
And make it happen.

It's hard to be
A calm, strong voice
That simply says,
"I believe
It can be done."

They're going to laugh.
They're going to scorn.
They're going to
Shake their heads.

Until they see someone
Turn on the light
And let it shine
And show a better way.

It takes courage
To stand alone
When no one else
Seems to care.

*H*ope swells my sail.

James Montgomery

A Candle in My Hand

Into each hand God has placed a candle. A simple candle with neither fancy ornaments nor special design. The purpose of a candle is to shed light. Light will give hope and illuminate the uneven path that lies ahead, both for myself and for others.

God gave us each a candle and he lit it.

Then the neighbor boy yelled and screamed and called me ugly names, and my light flickered and blinked for a bit. But soon the candle regained its flame, and the wick burned on. I still held it high.

I met a lot of teachers. Most were kind and thoughtful. But then came a teacher who put labels on my shoulders. She called me slow and shy and clumsy. For a while my light went out, and I stumbled in the darkness.

Fortunately God sent others to reignite that forgotten light. Out of the shadows, I could see clearly again. The flame helped me, and I shared it with others.

As a teen my light went crazy. One minute the flame was large and glowing. The next minute I could barely find a struggling spark. But fortunately God kept my light alive.

Eventually I married, and my spouse brought along a candle. Her candle beamed when mine burned low. The children came and went. We laughed and cried.

Through it all I knew that God handed me a candle. And if I didn't always see the light, at least I always knew it could be lit again. Sometimes God would light it. Other times a friend or relative provided the match. Many times I struggled to my feet and smacked flint stones together and found a spark myself.

The flame may come and go, but one thing has always remained the same: I know God gave me a candle.

*W*hen you say a situation or a
person is hopeless, you are slamming
the door in the face of God.

Charles L. Allen

The Lord is good to those whose hope is in him, to the one who seeks him.

Hope is a necessity for normal life,
and the major weapon against the suicide
  impulse.
Hope is not identical with optimism.
Optimism is distant from reality;
like pessimism, it emphasizes the importance of
  "I."
Hope is modest, humble, selfless; it implies
  progress;
it is an adventure, a going forward—
a confident search for a rewarding life.

                                    Dr. Karl Menninger

You Lift Me Up

I'd like to be that strong, independent type. The kind you read about and see in the movies. Someone who doesn't need anyone else, who rides out all the storms alone and bounces back from any kind of adversity. But truth be known, that isn't me. In my hours of disappointment I'm very glad to know you're there.

You lift me up.

Most folks think that a person who admits he or she needs other people is a marshmallow. So put me in a bag, seal it up, and mark it $1.39. I'm a marshmallow. I need someone to share coffee with. Someone to hear about my victories, my battles, and my defeats. I also need to hear someone else's experiences. Your stories keep me in touch with reality.

You lift me up.

And when I hear how happy you were or how much you enjoyed the afternoon with the family, my heart smiles along with yours. I watch your eyes dance as you talk. I watch your grin break against your cheeks. Rising and falling like a heart monitor, your joyful face tells half the story.

You lift me up.

If you weren't there, I would survive, even if I don't know how. I do know that when we are together I rise to a higher level. My today is livelier. My tomorrow is brighter. All because you are close at hand.

You lift me up.

So I thank God for you. Not out of obligation. Not with empty words. I thank God for you because you give me a reason to drink deeply from the well of life. With you I do not sample life or merely sip it now and again. I drink deeply because God has shown me his love in your eyes.

You lift me up.

In all the wedding cake,
hope is the sweetest of the plums.

Douglas Jerrold

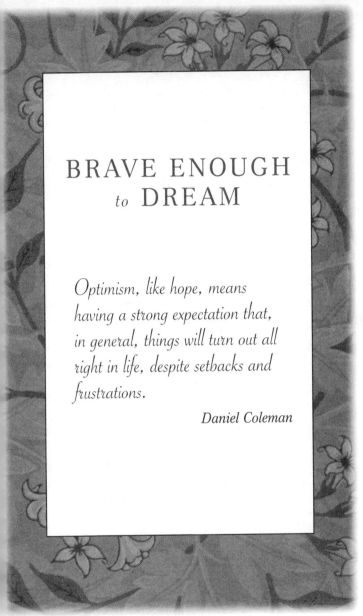

BRAVE ENOUGH
to DREAM

*Optimism, like hope, means
having a strong expectation that,
in general, things will turn out all
right in life, despite setbacks and
frustrations.*

Daniel Coleman

Help for a Sick Soul

Who among us has not had the feeling? A distinct sad feeling that the soul has become sick and frail. As if that inner person has gone to bed ill and lacks the strength and courage to rise up again.

A soul sickness is just as real as any physical illness. It's as if the heart were racked with fever. As if the spirit were aching or the mind clammy and weak. Souls are naturally robust, but poorly cared for, they quickly become anemic and pale.

The healthy soul must have *purpose*. It must rise up in the morning knowing why it's here. The good soul reaches out and touches other souls. By helping, encouraging, and caring for others the soul is fed and remains alive.

Each quiet soul must feed on *hope*. If it feeds on despair the inner person will grow emaciated. Hopelessness is like a diet of pop and candy. Without true nutritional value, our resources will dwindle and rot.

Hope, plans, and expectations cause the soul to sing. To give up hope would be like pouring cement over the garden of the soul.

As a well needs water, so a soul needs *challenge*. Souls do not prosper on yesterday's goals. What is it that we have yet to do? Is there a new bridge to cross? Is there another hill to climb? The healthy soul makes an effort to expand and not to shrivel.

Sometimes we can almost hear God saying aloud, "Rise up old soul and live again."

Turning to that tired, inactive soul, we call for it to find its way back. So we feed it. Morsel by morsel we offer our souls purpose, hope, and challenge. There are too many good things in life to let our souls roll over and die.

What is faith?
It is the confident assurance
that something we want is going to
  happen.
It is the certainty that what we hope
  for is waiting for us,
even though we cannot see it up
  ahead.

HEBREWS 11:1, TLB

This Weak Heart

If this weak heart
But had its choice,

I'd hear this night
My Savior's voice.

And soaring swift
Through time and space,

I'd see this night
My Savior's face.

*W*ithout hope
    men are only half alive.
With hope
    they dream and think and work.

Charles Sawyer

A Time for Heroes

Frequently the newspaper carries stories about sports figures who are selfish and immoral guys.

Fortunately there are also stories about athletes who are faithful spouses and sacrificing heroes. Chris Spielman, a linebacker for the Buffalo Bills, is a knight in padded gear.

A neck injury forced Spielman to sit out half the football season, but he was looking forward to returning to the team. That's when the bad news came about his wife, Stephanie. Doctors' reports said she had breast cancer, and the next six months would have to be dedicated to painful and difficult treatments.

How did this veteran football star react? He quit his job so he could dedicate the next half a year to his wife's recovery.

Chris and Stephanie bonded together to face the future and take on its challenges.

When the going gets tough, the tough don't run away from the people they love.

Almost all of us have something rough waiting down the road. So do the people we care about.

Health problems will come. The phone will ring in the middle of the night. E-mail will bring sad news. Death will eventually pay a call. The future will bring its own bad news.

Those are the times for common heroes—the ones who stick in there when the storm is raging. There are plenty of people who enter relationships only to jump ship at the first sign of severe weather. Heroes stay to guide the ship, bail water, and speak words of encouragement.

The future does not call for fictional heroes who wrestle lions or stop speeding trains. True heroes fix meals, hold hands, bring washcloths, and give rides to the hospital. True heroes say "I love you" when they turn out the light at night.

Heroes seldom get their names in the newspaper. Not on the business page, the sports page, or the criminal records. Their real value lies in the quiet way they love, care, and make the day brighter.

No, in all these things we are more than conquerors through him who loved us. For I am convinced that neither death nor life, neither angels nor demons, neither the present nor the future, nor any powers, neither height nor depth, nor anything else in all creation, will be able to separate us from the love of God that is in Christ Jesus our Lord.

ROMANS 8:37-39

Great ideas come into the world
 as gently as doves.
Perhaps, then, if we listen attentively,
we shall hear, amid the uproar of
 empires and nations,
a faint flutter of wings,
the gentle stirrings of life and hope.

Albert Camus

Against all hope,
Abraham in hope believed
and so became the father of many
    nations,
just as it had been said of him,
    "So shall your offspring be."

ROMANS 4:18

Working for Good

An armed robber brandishing a drawn gun entered the small cafe. People dashed to the corners of the room or hid under tables. As the clerk filled a sack with money, fear hung throughout the room. Some prayed, some wept. The great majority kept their faces covered.

Shouting threats, the thief moved toward the door. At the exit he paused long enough to arbitrarily shoot one of the crouching diners. A bullet pierced the man's side, leaving him severely wounded.

In that single moment the victim's entire life was changed drastically. The pain, the race to the hospital, the emergency surgery all blurred with the sound of screams, sirens, slamming doors, and bright lights.

Recuperation and rehabilitation took months, but eventually he returned to a fairly normal life. Looking back at that terrifying event the man made this surprising observation: Almost every part of the horrible experience worked toward something good coming into his life.

He found himself returning to the faith of his

childhood. He met new friends that otherwise he would never have known. Soon he became more active with the family he had long ignored. He considered each day valuable and established new goals.

There is no way he would volunteer to repeat the near-death tragedy. However, he is tremendously thankful for the many good things that came from it. Being shot during a totally illogical holdup worked its way into benefits he would not have imagined.

His new life became the embodiment of the thought expressed in Romans 8:28: "And we know that in all things God works for the good of those who love him, who have been called according to his purpose."

None of us will look for someone to shoot us. Our new theme will not be "Better living by being gunned down." But this man's story reflects a broad Christian principle: When terrible things come our way, our faith helps us look for any and all the good we can find. And usually we will find it.

Christians don't have to pretend that good will be there. If we look closely, it actually does exist. That's real faith working in a real way.

A continual looking forward to the eternal world is not (as some modern people think) a form of escapism or wishful thinking, but one of the things a Christian is meant to do.

C.S. Lewis

You are in seven times greater danger
of becoming a millionaire than you are
of being struck by lightning.
Good things are far more likely to
happen to us than bad things.

Dreaming Is an Illness

Choosing to dream
Is an irrational act.

Why would anyone care
To let his mind
Fly about the room
And soar around
The countryside?

What fool would dare
To picture
A better day,
An exciting tomorrow,
A brighter road
To travel?

Dreaming is an illness,
After all.

Dreaming is contagious;
It causes others to dream.
Dreaming is a vision;
It causes us to see beyond.
Dreaming is a fever;
It says something else
Is going on.

Who would care to see
How much better things
Could be
And dare to try
To make those dreams
Come true?

And who would leave
His comfort zone
To make his dreams
Come true?

Dreaming is an illness,
After all.

The Thought of Heaven

With so many good things and bad things in the present life, we seldom pause and take time to think about heaven. However, it is our failure to think about the afterlife that makes the present life considerably more difficult.

Heaven is the ultimate hope. Daily hopes pale when measured against the Big Hope.

We know so little about heaven that our imaginations must fill in the blanks. However, there are some hints.

For instance, that no-tears clause in Revelation 21:4. This alone should make us eager to reach our destination. No taxes, no gallstones, and no dentists (to be sure, dentists will be allowed into heaven, but they have to check their drills in at the gate).

No crying also means no hunger, no hatred, no cancer, and no separation. No crying on the outside, no weeping on the inside.

What about activities? Because people in coffins don't move around, we seem to assume heaven is one gigantic nap. Let's fill in this blank with people

busily worshiping, sharing, helping others, playing tennis, and painting clouds. However, my imagination refuses to picture meetings or committees.

Apparently there is a good supply of music: voices, instruments, and sextets everywhere. Don't limit the scene to harps and classical music, but throw in guitars, drums, and a synthesizer. We may have to negotiate the volume level when we get there.

Mainly there will be lots of people. All kinds of people. The child who left us too early. Friends who departed abruptly. Grandparents who sailed away in their sleep. Spouses who took our hearts with them. I imagine a lot of hugging goes on.

The biggest attraction in the sky won't be the Milky Way or Jupiter; it will be God himself. His presence, his majesty, his love will seem overwhelming. When we see his Son face to face we'll be able to thank him for living and dying for us.

We are left to our imaginations. We couldn't begin to grasp the reality. Heaven is too splendid, too different, too wonderful, too much. It overflows with hope.

I know the world is filled with troubles
   and many injustices.
But reality is as beautiful as it is ugly.
I think it is just as important to sing
about beautiful mornings as it is to talk
   about slums.
I just couldn't write anything without
   hope in it.

Oscar Hammerstein II

*B*e joyful in hope,
patient in affliction,
faithful in prayer.

ROMANS 12:12